my friend is s

Thoughts of Suicide

**Josh McDowell
& Ed Stewart**

WORD PUBLISHING

NASHVILLE

A Thomas Nelson Company

Scripture quotations used in this book are from the Holy Bible, New International Version. Copyright © 1973, 1978, 1984, International Bible Society. Used by permission of Zondervan Bible Publishers.

Library of Congress Cataloging-in-Publication Data

McDowell, Josh.
    My friend is struggling with—thoughts of suicide / by
Josh McDowell and Ed Stewart.
    p. cm. — (Project 911 collection)
    Summary: Uses the story of a teenage boy who is worried
about a friend to explore the problem of suicide and what to do for
someone who has suicidal thoughts.
    ISBN 0-8499-3792-2
    1. Youth—Suicidal behavior—Prevention—Juvenile litera
ture. 2. Suicide—Juvenile literature. 3. Suicide—Prevention—
Juvenile literature. [1. Suicide. 2. Christian life.] I. Stewart,
Ed. II. Title. III. Series.
    HV6546 .M39 2000
    362.28—dc21

00-028110

CIP

Printed in the United States of America

00 01 02 03 04 05 QDT 9 8 7 6 5 4 3 2 1

Acknowledgments

We would like to thank the following people:

David Ferguson, director of Intimate Life Ministries of Austin, Texas, has made a tremendous contribution to this collection. David's influence, along with the principles of the Intimate Life message, is felt throughout each book in this collection. David has modeled before us how to be God's comfort, support, and encouragement to others. We encourage you to take advantage of the seminars and resources that Intimate Life Ministries offers. (See pages 49–54 for more information about how this ministry can serve you.)

Dave Bellis, my (Josh) associate of twenty-three years, labored with us to mold and shape

acknowledgments

each book in this collection. Each fictional story in all eight books in the PROJECT 911 collection was derived from the dramatic audio segments of the "Youth in Crisis Resource," which Dave personally wrote. He was also responsible for the design and coordination of the entire PROJECT 911 family of resources (see pages 56–59). We are so very grateful for Dave's talents and involvement.

Joey Paul of Word Publishing not only believed in this entire project, but also consistently championed it throughout Word.

JOSH MCDOWELL

ED STEWART

Sean's Story

The youth-group car wash raised $430 for summer church-camp scholarships, but it will probably be better remembered for the riotous water fight. During a lull in the parade of dirty cars, the high-school seniors, led by energetic Sean Williams, commandeered the two hoses and opened fire on the rest of the group. The underclassmen fought back gamely with buckets and sponges filled with soapy water.

Caught in no-man's land during the battle were youth-group sponsors Doug and Jenny Shaw. But the Shaws, who claimed to be "thirty-something," had come prepared. As soon as the water started flying, Doug pulled an arsenal of high-powered water guns from the trunk of his car, and he and Jenny opened fire on everyone. The good-natured, twenty-minute battle left the group drenched to the skin and sore from laughter. And the soaking seemed to refresh the crew for the last two hours of work in the hot afternoon sun.

Sean was among the last to leave after cleanup, conveniently "forgetting" to ask for a ride home with some of his friends in the group. He had planned it that way. As Sean and Doug were stowing the last of the cleaning supplies in the church storage room, Sean said, "Could I get a ride home with you and Jenny, if it's not too much trouble?"

Doug responded just as Sean had hoped. "Of course. No trouble at all."

Sean smiled to himself. Doug and Jenny Shaw were very special people in his life. They had supported him when he really needed someone. And he knew they would help him now with the burden he was carrying.

Doug suggested that they stop for burgers on the way home. Jenny and Sean wholeheartedly agreed, since they had been too busy washing cars—and spraying each other with water—to eat lunch.

"I need to talk to you two about something," Sean said soberly after they had placed their orders at the Burger Shack.

"I wondered if you had something on your mind," Jenny said. "You've been a little quieter than normal—except during today's water fight, of course."

Sean smiled briefly then returned to his concern. "It's kind of serious, and I'm not sure what to do. So I'm hoping you have some suggestions."

Doug flashed an assuring smile. "We are more than happy to listen and help if we can, Sean."

The waitress arrived with their drinks. Sean stirred his Coke gently with a straw as he composed his thoughts. "I'm worried about my friend Kev," he said at last.

"Kev . . . you mean Kevin Colvin?" Jenny probed. "The guy who comes to church with you sometimes?"

"Kevin—right. A lot of us call him Kev. His parents are not Christians, but he says he trusts

Christ as his Savior. Lately he's been acting strange."

"Is Kevin in some kind of trouble?" Doug asked.

Sean released a long sigh. "I don't know for sure. He's been really quiet and distant for the last few weeks. And I've noticed a few other things about him that worry me."

Doug leaned a little closer. "Like what?"

Sean felt odd talking about something that stirred up such painful memories. But he knew he had to for his friend's sake. "Well, things that make me wonder if Dannie has thought about suicide."

Jenny reached across the table and touched his arm. "This must be difficult for you, Sean. I'm sorry you have to deal with this issue again after what you have been through."

Sean felt a lump in his throat. He remembered all too clearly his bout with depression two years earlier that pushed him to gulp down a fistful of sleeping pills. But Doug and Jenny had been there to help him through. Sean would be forever grateful for the love and concern this couple had shown in his darkest hour.

"Thanks. I think I'm doing all right," he said, clearing his throat. "But I'm afraid for Kev. His parents are too busy fighting to pay much attention to him. His older brothers have moved away, so he's all alone at home. And when his friend Tim died in a car crash this spring, he really began to withdraw. I'm worried about him."

Doug spoke next. "What else is Kev doing that makes you suspect he may have thought about suicide?"

"Some things that are painfully familiar. Kev seems tired all the time—he has no energy. If I call him at noon on a Saturday, he's still in bed. Even when I talk him into coming over, he just wants to flop in a corner and go to sleep."

"Fatigue was one of the symptoms that concerned us about you," Jenny said.

Sean nodded. "I'm glad you noticed," he said softly. "Kev is also getting into black stuff—clothes, leather, jewelry—and talking like he's fascinated with death. He's been real moody too—angry one minute, silent the next."

"I'm so glad that you have been paying attention to Kev's behavior, Sean," Jenny affirmed. "He seems to be crying out for help."

The waitress arrived with their burgers and fries. In his prayer of thanks for the food, Doug also prayed for Kevin.

As they began to eat, Sean continued. "The thing that really bothers me is that Kev has been giving stuff away—even some great stuff, like his mountain bike. He doesn't seem to care about anything. It's like he's not planning to stay around much longer."

Doug and Jenny wore expressions of obvious concern. Sean felt better that he had shared his worries with them.

After taking one bite, Doug set his hamburger down. "Sean, do you know if Kev has ever attempted suicide before?"

"I don't think so."

"Have you heard Kev actually say he wants to commit suicide?" Doug went on.

Sean shook his head. "I'm not with him all

the time, of course. But he has never said anything like that to me."

"Have you seen any kind of a suicide note he may be working on?" Doug said.

"No, nothing like that."

Jenny asked, "Do you know what to do if he attempts suicide when you are around?"

Sean was silent for a moment. "I would do what my mom and you did for me," he said soberly. "I would get him to an emergency room right away. I would not leave him for a minute until he was in the care of a doctor."

The flashback was chillingly clear. One moment Sean was gulping down pills. The next moment—or so it seemed in his memory—he was in the emergency room with a tube down his throat. His mom and Doug and Jenny were there too, crying and praying. Sean's mother had called the Shaws in a panic when she discovered the empty bottle and could not rouse her sleeping son. The youth sponsors had rushed to meet them at the hospital and stayed with Sean until he was out of danger.

"And if Kev threatens suicide or if you find a

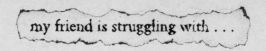
suicide note," Jenny continued, "do you know what to do?"

Sean responded, "Call for help right away. Stay with him until he is in the care of a mental-health professional."

"That's right," Jenny said. "I expected you knew, but I wanted to hear you say it. Do you feel okay about taking such serious steps?"

"Absolutely," Sean said without hesitation. "Kev is my friend, and I don't want him to die. I'll do anything I can to help him. After all, someone loved me enough to help me."

Jenny touched Sean's arm again. "Doug and I thank God that you got to the hospital in time. We love you. You are very special to us."

Sean smiled and nodded at his friends. "Thanks, both of you. I'm sure I'll do the right thing if Kev really tries to kill himself. But I don't want to wait until the last minute to help him. So what can I do?"

"It's interesting that you would ask that question, Sean," Doug began. "After your episode with the pills two years ago, Jenny and I realized that we did not know much about the warning signs for suicide. We were rather naive. We had heard the statistics: One thousand teenage students attempt suicide every day in our country, and eighteen actually succeed. But we didn't think it was a problem believers would face."

Jenny picked up the explanation. "Doug and I realize now that kids are kids, whether they are Christians or not. Lots of kids suffer from stress, unfulfilled needs, and loneliness. Some kids live in families scarred by separation, divorce, and rejection. Some experience clinical depression. Others feel trapped in seemingly hopeless situations and are looking for an easy way out. Many kids today are seriously starved for attention, and they will try anything to get it—even suicide. Doug and I have learned to watch for the warning signs and to treat the cause, not just the symptoms."

"That's what I want to do for Kev," Sean insisted. "Will you help me?"

"Of course," Doug assured him. "Let us share with you a few key concepts we have learned over the last two years."

By the time the trio finished their burgers, Sean had received several helpful tips for responding to Kevin's suspicious behavior. Doug concluded their chat by reassuring Sean. "We really admire your concern and commitment to help Kevin. And we want you to know that we're here for you as you help him. Feel free to tell us how it's going and to call on us for help. We will be praying for you—and for Kev."

That night Sean lay awake thinking about what Doug and Jenny had said. It was good advice, and he prayed that God would help him apply it in his friendship with Kev. And he prayed hard that Kev would not try anything foolish before he was able to show his friend how much he cared for him.

Time Out to Consider

Perhaps, like Sean, you have noticed disturbing behavior in a friend. You can't quite put your finger on the problem, but you find yourself wondering if your friend is thinking about suicide. Your concern is worth considering because suicide is the second-leading cause of death among students today. Research confirms that a staggering sixty-five hundred teenagers die each year at their own hands—that's one every hour and twenty minutes! If your friend is exhibiting potentially suicidal behavior, now is the time to do something to make sure he or she does not follow through with that impulse.

There are three degrees of severity when discussing suicide.

First, there are kids who actually *attempt* suicide. If you happen to be around when someone attempts to take his or her own life, you have only one response: Call 911 or a responsible adult and get that person to an emergency room or mental-health hospital *immediately*. This person needs professional help to prevent him or her from making another attempt.

Second, there are kids who *threaten or seriously contemplate* suicide. If you discover a suicide note or learn that a friend is seriously thinking about suicide, you must act to intervene. Contact a youth leader, minister, or parent—someone who can get your friend to a Christian counseling professional. Do not leave your friend alone until he or she is in the care of a responsible adult. Threats of suicide must be regarded as potential attempts.

Third, there are kids like Kevin Colvin who have *passing thoughts* about suicide. This may be your concern for your friend. Like Kevin, your friend may exhibit certain symptoms of suicidal thinking. If you can answer yes to any of the following questions, your friend may be on the threshold of seriously contemplating suicide:

1. Does your friend have an unhealthy fascination with death—talking about death, asking questions about death, listening to music or watching videos related to death or dying?

2. Is your friend giving away possessions, cleaning out his or her locker at school, or doing other things that suggest he or she is preparing for death?

3. Is your friend depressed most of the time?

4. Has your friend exhibited sudden changes in behavior, such as acting out or becoming violent?

5. Is your friend often moody, sullen, or with-drawn?

6. Does your friend want to sleep all the time, or does he or she complain about not being able to sleep?

7. Is your friend often fatigued?

8. Does your friend take dangerous risks, such as driving recklessly or playing with knives or guns?

While these conditions do not necessarily mean that your friend is about to commit suicide, they may indicate that he or she is thinking about it as a way out. You are wise to do as Sean did: Share your concerns with your youth leader, minister, or parent, and discuss what to do. Now is the time to respond proactively.

What kinds of problems are behind these tell-tale signs? What prompts a student to consider committing suicide? Here are several possible situations that may cause a person to think dying is preferable to living. One or more of them may be at the root of your friend's disturbing behavior.

Family disruption. How is your friend's family life? Is he or she suffering from a sense of alienation or parental rejection? Sean mentioned that Kevin's parents fight and his older brothers have moved away. The stress and loneliness that accompany divorce or separation, a drastic move, or ongoing family conflict may trigger thoughts of suicide.

Depression. Does your friend seem to be depressed most of the time? Clinical depression is an illness that often prevents people from seeing a way out of their problems. Without proper professional treatment, victims of depression may see suicide as their only alternative.

Escape. Does your friend seem to feel trapped in a seemingly hopeless situation? Suicide is often viewed by students as an escape from despair, pain, punishment, humiliation, or simply the weight of mental and emotional burdens.

Loss. Has your friend suffered the tragic loss of a parent, close friend, or loved one? Sean said that Kevin was disturbed over the recent death of a friend in a car accident. Suicide may be regarded as a way to escape the seemingly unbearable sorrow and grief of such a loss.

Guilt. Is your friend burdened with guilt over something he or she has done? Suicide is sometimes entertained as the ultimate punishment for what the person considers to be an unforgivable act.

Attention or manipulation. Does your friend feel unimportant and ignored by parents, peers, or friends? If so, threats or attempts at suicide are often a cry for attention and for help. It may be your friend's way of saying, "I'm hurting. I'm desperate. I don't know how to cope, and I need help. Please, someone pay attention to me!" Suicidal threats may also be an attempt to manipulate parents into giving him or her something he or she wants.

Revenge. Has your friend been severely hurt or embarrassed by someone? Sometimes the desire for revenge is stronger than the desire to live. Self-destruction is seen as the ultimate act of punishment against the hurtful person. Suicidal revenge may be the twisted response to the breakup of a close emotional relationship.

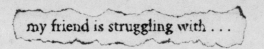

If you have a friend like Kevin who is show-ing subtle clues of suicide, there is hope. You can take some positive steps toward relieving the pain that may be causing your friend to entertain thoughts of suicide. Hopefully, you have the prayerful support and guidance of adults like Doug and Jenny, mature Christians on whom you may call if you need help. But even if you don't, you can be a great help to your friend, just as Sean is about to be with Kevin.

Sean's Story

It seemed to take forever for Sean to find some-thing Kevin would do with him. They used to enjoy biking together, until Sean's friend shocked him by giving away an expensive mountain bike. Every other idea—playing video games, going to the gym, going to the batting cages—was met with words like "I don't think so" or "I'm too tired."

But when Sean suggested that they speed skate the paved path along the river, Kev showed a spark of interest. So Sean arrived at Kev's house at 10:00 on a sunny Saturday morning to get him out of bed and help him find his roller blades and kneepads in the garage. By 11:30, they were gliding along the neighborhood sidewalks at high speed toward the river.

Kev didn't talk much as they raced along the tree-lined path. Sean, who was a better skater, let his friend lead. Following Kev, Sean prayed that God would increase his compassion for his friend and give him words that would help unlock Kev's disturbing behavior.

Reaching the halfway point, Kev was out of breath. So Sean suggested that they catch a breath near the path and sip some water. Kev quickly agreed. They flipped off their kneepads and collapsed on a bench facing the river.

"This is really cool, Kev," Sean said, passing a water bottle to his friend. "We haven't done anything like this in a long time."

"Yeah, I know," Kev said, breathing hard. He took a swallow and stared out at the river. Sean regarded his friend's appearance. He wore faded black shorts and a ragged black T-shirt emblazoned with the image of a rock group posed in a cemetery. His sad-looking face and hollow eyes were framed by stringy dark hair. Kev used to be more conscientious about his appearance, even when doing something athletic. Sean felt sad because his friend didn't seem to care about himself anymore.

Encouraged by his talk with Doug and Jenny, Sean decided to break the ice. "Kev, I've been wanting to talk to you about something," he began cautiously.

Kev continued to gaze out at the river, saying nothing.

Sean continued. "We haven't been doing as much stuff together lately. Is everything all right . . . I mean, with us?"

Kev shrugged. "Yeah, everything is okay I guess."

"It just seems like you haven't wanted to do much lately."

"I've been kind of busy and kind of tired."

Sean paused, hoping he didn't sound too nosy. Then he added, "You've also seemed a little quiet and a little down. Is everything else all right?"

Kev didn't answer for several moments. Then he finally looked at Sean. "Not exactly," he said at last, a shadow of pain drifting across his face.

"Is there something I can help you with?" Sean probed.

Kev looked away again, then he dropped his head and stared at the ground. Finally he said, "Not unless you can keep my parents from getting a divorce or turn all my Fs into Cs at school."

"Your parents are getting a divorce?" Sean said with surprise.

Kev nodded slowly. "Mom found out Dad has a 'girlfriend' at the office. So she kicked him out and told him she didn't even want him to see me. It's been awful at our house."

Sean touched his friend's shoulder. "Man, Kev, I'm so sorry. I knew your mom and dad were having trouble. But divorce . . . that must really hurt."

Head drooping low, Kev blinked hard a couple of times and rubbed his nose. Sean had never seen his friend look so sad. He felt a lump of sorrow for him swelling in his throat.

"If you want to tell me about it," Sean went on, "I'll be glad to listen."

Kev glanced at him almost scornfully. "You don't need to do that, Sean."

"What do you mean?"

"I mean you don't have to get involved. You have your own problems to deal with. You don't need to hear about mine."

"Kev, we're friends and I—"

"So we go biking and skating sometimes," Kev interrupted. "That doesn't mean you have to take on my problems."

"Hey, we're friends, remember?" Sean said. "If you're bummed out and there is something I can do to help, I'm here—even if it just means listening to you."

Kev turned back toward the river, thinking. Sean prayed silently for his friend.

"It may be too late to help me," Kev said, just above a whisper.

The words sent a chill down Sean's spine. "What do you mean?"

"I mean, what's the point? My parents hate each other, and they can't stand me. My brothers think I'm a pest. I'm screwing up in all my classes. My best friend Tim was killed, and my friends don't want to hang out with me—except for you."

"You really miss Tim, don't you?" Sean said. "I'm so sad that you feel alone. And I didn't realize school was difficult for you right now too. I'm so sorry, Kev."

Kev released a sharp sigh. Sean could see the pain in his face. "I'm just a waste of space on this planet, and I'm so tired of being in the way."

Sean jabbed his elbow at his friend. "You are *not* a waste of space," he insisted. "You are a child of God. You are a guy with really great gifts. Whenever you feel like a waste of space, you just call me, and I'll remind you how good you are. And there is nothing happening in your life that you and I and the Lord can't get through together. Remember, God loves you, and I think you're okay too, except you're such a lousy skater."

Kev chuckled under his breath as he placed his hand on Sean's shoulder. "Thanks, man," Kevin said, almost in a whisper. After a few moments of silence, Kev began to describe how much he hurt about his parents splitting up about the same time his friend had died. He said he had a stomachache almost all the time and that he just wanted to sleep. Since he was unable to concentrate, his grades had suffered terribly. Kev didn't think that he would ever catch up in school, nor did he feel it was worth trying.

"I'm really bummed for you, Kev. I know it's got to be tough with your folks splitting up and all." Sean looked straight ahead. He tapped his friend's knee with his fist as he spoke. "It hurts me that you have to go through all this stuff. I wish you didn't have to hurt like this."

Kev also spoke about feeling rejected by his brothers and the loneliness of being without his friends. "I know it's tough," Sean assured him. "But we're friends, and we'll get through all this." Then Sean prayed a simple prayer for Kevin just loud enough for God and his friend to hear.

After a few more minutes of comforting Kev, Sean said, "Why don't we skate to the end of the path and eat?"

Following Kev again, Sean thanked God silently for the opportunity to comfort his friend. He knew that their brief time on the riverside bench was only a beginning. But Sean was encouraged to continue with the suggestions Doug and Jenny had provided.

When they reached the end of the path, Sean unloaded his small backpack and spread out the sandwiches he had packed for both of them. The two pulled off their skates and socks and dipped their feet in the river as they ate sandwiches and tortilla chips. The gentle breeze off the river felt refreshing. Sean noticed that Kev's face was a little brighter, and he knew it was more than just the sunshine.

"Hey, I'm serious," Sean said with a mouth full of chips. "I want to know what's happening with you and school. What classes are giving you the most trouble? How far behind are you?"

Kev groaned at the reminder of his scholastic embarrassment. "I guess you can't keep secrets from friends, can you?" he said wryly.

"I'm not trying to rub it in," Sean interjected quickly. "You know, maybe I can help."

"There's only a month left in the semester, Sean," Kev said. "Even the world's fastest computer couldn't dig me out of this hole." He went on to explain that he was failing in biology and American lit, and barely hovering above failure in three other classes. He had missed a number of homework assignments, which had left him unprepared for several exams he had either failed or nearly failed.

Sean listened intently. Then he said, "Maybe we can't pull all your grades up to As or Bs. But I'll bet we can pull most of them up to Cs. At least you'll pass. How does that sound?"

"You want to help me get my grades up?" Kev said with a look of disbelief. "Why? Do you like schoolwork that much?"

Sean smiled. "You know better than that. It's just that I want to help, that's all. That's what friends are for. I know some other kids at church who would be willing to help too."

"You guys would be willing to cheat for me?"

"I'm not talking about doing your work for you," Sean explained. "I'm talking about helping you sort through your missing assignments and stuff to get you caught up. And studying together for tests, things like that."

"Kind of like tutoring," Kev put in.

"Right. I do pretty well in the lit and history areas, so I can help you there. Rachel DeWitt is a math and science expert, so she could probably help you catch up in biology. What do you think?"

"Rachel's cool. I like her," Kev responded.

The two were silent for several moments. "I don't know what to think," Kevin began. "Nobody's offered to help me like this, not even my parents—at least, not since Tim died. I've pretty much felt like I was in it alone—you know, sink or swim, get with the program or get out of the way. It was getting harder and harder to stay afloat in school and at home."

"Well, it's not like that anymore, Kev," Sean assured him. "I'm sorry it took me so long to realize how tough things were getting for you. But I want to help. I know others in the youth group do too, including Doug and Jenny. Is that okay with you?"

Kev smiled. "Yeah," he said at last, "that's okay with me. Thanks . . . friend."

Kev seemed happier and more animated during the skate back home. Sean also noticed a

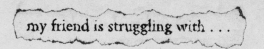

burst of energy in his friend that at times made it difficult for him to keep up. It was good to see Kev open up and brighten up.

Sean decided he would call his friend or spend time with him at school each day, just to touch base and show his interest. And whenever the weather cooperated, Sean intended to get Kev out skating on the riverside path.

Time Out to Consider

Watching Sean and Kev during their day of skating, you may have an idea about how Doug and Jenny counseled Sean to deal with his depressed and despairing friend. If your friend is displaying signs of hopelessness or despair, you can follow the Shaws' advice too. Your response to your friend may not look exactly like Sean's response to Kevin, but there are at least four key elements you should consider when trying to help your friend.

Here is a word of caution first. Thoughts of suicide and the conditions or attitudes that provoke them in a young person's life are serious business. Sean did a wise thing by seeking advice from Doug and Jenny Shaw. You would also be wise to seek the counsel, encouragement, and prayer support of a parent, youth leader, or minister as you deal with your friend, even if you feel very confident to minister to him or her. If you do not feel confident in this situation, ask a mature Christian to help you. And if you sense at any point that your friend needs more help than you can provide, be sure to enlist the assistance of a Christian leader or minister.

Provide a caring relationship for your friend. People who entertain passing thoughts of suicide usually feel very alone inside. Whether they are social loners or very socially active, they often hurt for lack of someone who cares deeply about them, invests time in them, and regards them as significant. Kevin Colvin is a good example. Problems at home involving his parents left him feeling unwanted and abandoned. The death of his friend Tim left him feeling very alone. And when these pressures caused his studies to suffer, Kev felt alienated from his friends at school, who avoided him. Someone who is alone and feeling unloved can easily begin to feel, as Kevin did, that he or she is just taking up space.

The most important thing you can share with someone battling the despair of loneliness is yourself. Potentially suicidal persons need to build strong, open relationships with others. Sean and Kevin already had a relationship as friends. But Kevin's problems had caused him to pull away. During their meeting together, Doug and Jenny encouraged Sean to take the initiative for deepening the relationship. If you are committed to helping your friend move beyond thoughts of suicide, it may cost you some time and energy as you seek to meet his or her need for love and friendship.

Here are several ways to develop a caring relationship that will help your friend feel less alone:

1. *Be concerned for your friend.* The best way to deal with a person who may be entertaining thoughts of suicide is to demonstrate your interest and concern. Sean showed his concern for Kevin by going to Doug and Jenny

for input on how to help. If you know that your friend is hurting, allow your heart to be moved with concern to the point that you act.

2. *Be available to your friend.* For most hurting people, love is spelled T-I-M-E. Sean took time out of his schedule to go skating with Kevin and to engage him in conversation. Look for opportunities to spend time with your friend in order to build your relationship.

3. *Keep in touch with your friend.* An occasional phone call just to say hello and to ask how your friend is doing shows that you care even when you are not doing something together.

4. *Pray for your friend.* Ask God to show you ways to build your relationship and meet some of your friend's needs for love and acceptance.

5. *Affirm your friend's identity as a child of God.* Suicidal persons have lost sight of their value and worth to God. If your friend is a Christian, remind him or her that he or she is loved, valued, and useful to God. If your friend is not a Christian, that person is still

created in God's image, someone for whom Christ died. Look for ways to affirm your friend's value and worth to God.

6. *Try to instill hope in your friend.* Kevin had lost hope, seeing himself as a waste of space on the planet. Like most kids who consider suicide, he was not evaluating his life or processing his problems rationally. The best way to instill hope in such persons is by focusing on feelings instead of arguing over how they think. Sean communicated hope by feeling Kevin's sorrow with him and by comforting him. Once hope is restored, there will be time to deal with your friend's irrational view of his or her situation.

7. *Talk with your friend.* Sean discovered that Kevin really didn't have anyone to talk to. Many discouraged, depressed students report that they cannot talk to their parents about problems, hurts, and decisions. Encourage your friend to talk to you about his or her life and difficulties. Be sure to respect your friend's opinions without judgment or con-

demnation, even if they are questionable. It is very important that your friend feel free to verbalize his or her feelings to someone who cares.

As you try to deepen your relationship with your friend in these ways, consider three more vital steps to helping him or her overcome thoughts of suicide.

Comfort your hurting friend. Kevin's primary need in the midst of his emotional pain and loneliness was comfort. That is why Sean identified with Kevin's hurt on the riverside bench. Jesus said, "Blessed are those who mourn, for they will be comforted" (Matt. 5:4). Mourning is the process of getting the inner hurt out. In response to Sean's gentle questions, Kevin "mourned" his painful situation at home and at school. As he admitted how sad he felt, Sean was able to share in that pain too. According to Jesus' words, when Sean comforted his friend, Kevin was "blessed." Comfort is God's design for blessing those who hurt and for beginning to heal the deep pain of being alone and feeling hopeless.

In the midst of trouble, anxiety, and thoughts of suicide, your friend's greatest comfort will come when you share his or her hurt and sorrow. One major way God shares His comfort with others is through us. The apostle Paul wrote, "God . . . comforts us in all our troubles, so that we can comfort those in any trouble with the comfort we ourselves have received from God" (2 Cor. 1:3, 4). Comfort is not a "pep talk" urging your friend to hang in there, to tough it out, or to hold it together. Comfort is not an attempt to explain why things happen to people. Comfort is not a bunch of positive words about God being in control and everything being okay. All of these things may be good and useful in time, but they do not fill the primary need for comfort.

People receive comfort when we feel their hurt and sorrow with them. Jesus illustrated the ministry of comfort when His friend Lazarus died (see John 11). When Jesus arrived at the home of Lazarus's sisters, Mary and Martha, He wept with them (see vv. 33–35). His response is especially interesting in light of what He did next: raise Lazarus from the dead (see vv. 38–44).

Why didn't Jesus simply tell the grieving Mary and Martha, "No need to cry, My friends, because in a few minutes Lazarus will be alive again"? Because at that moment they needed someone to identify with their sorrow. Jesus met Mary's and Martha's need for comfort by sharing in their sorrow and tears. Later He performed the miracle that turned their sorrows to joy.

Hurting people receive comfort when they know they are not suffering alone. Paul instructed us, "Rejoice with those who rejoice; mourn with those who mourn" (Rom. 12:15). Others may try to comfort Kevin by cheering him up, urging him to be strong, or explaining the causes of his suicidal thoughts. These people may care about him and mean well by their words. But they may not know what comfort sounds like. The comfort Kevin needs is found in Sean's identifying with him emotionally.

You can comfort your hurting friend in the same way. Share in their hurt and struggles. Offer a gentle touch, an appropriate embrace, or a shoulder to cry on. Share words like, "I know it hurts," "I'm so sorry you have to go through this,"

"I really hurt for you." Save your words of advice or admonitions from Scripture until you have identified with your friend's feelings. That's biblical comfort.

Offer support to your friend. Your hurting friend needs support as well as comfort. What's the difference? You provide comfort when you share in your friend's sorrow emotionally. You provide support when you attempt to lighten your friend's load in practical, helpful ways. Even in the midst of pain and struggle, the day-to-day tasks of life go on. Things must be done that your friend may have difficulty doing. He or she needs someone who is committed to obeying Galatians 6:2: "Carry each other's burdens, and in this way you will fulfill the law of Christ."

Kevin not only needed comfort, but he also needed help with his schoolwork. Sean provided needed support when he volunteered to put together a small team of tutors who would help Kevin pull up his semester grades. Sean's support may also include such tasks as helping Kevin clean his room, find a part-time job, get a ride to church, or complete any number of practical tasks.

How can you be a helpful support to your suffering friend? Watch and ask questions. If you are aware of a task your friend is already doing, you can say, "May I help you with that?" If you don't see something obvious to do, ask, "Is there anything I can do to help you?" Ask others who know your friend to help share the load. Your support will ease the burden and allow your friend to concentrate on dealing with his or her emotional crisis.

Provide encouragement for your friend. We encourage others whenever we do or say something thoughtful to lift their spirits. After his day of skating and sharing with Kevin, Sean planned to call his friend periodically just to be available and to remind Kevin that he is thinking about him and praying for him. That's encouragement in action.

Your hurting friend needs encouragement as much as he or she needs comfort and support. Here are a few ideas.

- Send an occasional note or e-mail that communicates in your own words, "I care about you" and "I'm praying for you."

- Call your friend and say something like, "Hi, I just want you to know that I'm thinking about you."

- Take the initiative to schedule a time to meet for lunch or a Coke. Focus attention on how your friend is doing.

- If your friend is playing sports, performing in a play, or participating in a debate or some other activity, attend the event to show your support.

- Ask a few other mutual friends to join you in supplying the encouragement your friend needs.

Your thoughtful words and deeds of comfort, support, and encouragement will be an ongoing reminder to your friend that he or she is not alone. And when people with thoughts of suicide realize they are loved and cared for, they will begin to see themselves and their life situations in a healthier light.

Once you have initiated steps of comfort, support, and encouragement, you may have an opportunity to share with your friend more pointedly about his or her worth as a person. Sean had that opportunity just a couple of weeks after his conversation with Kevin beside the river.

Sean's Story

Sean and Kevin walked the seven blocks from the high school to Doug Shaw's house. Sean noted with secret delight that Kevin looked and sounded much better than he had two weeks earlier during their skate and chat. Sean had said nothing to his friend about his appearance, but Kevin's colorful clothes and hair showed that he was feeling much better about himself.

Only a few days after their Saturday skate together, Kevin had admitted what Sean had suspected. "You'll probably think I'm some kind of psycho," he'd said one day as they watched a

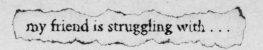

school volleyball match, "but I was beginning to wonder if my life was worth living. Compared to how bad things were, dying didn't seem too bad."

Sean comforted Kevin again and assured him that he was no "psycho." A few days later Sean asked if Kevin would like to meet with Doug Shaw, the youth-group sponsor, to talk about his problems at home. Kevin agreed—if Sean would go with him. Sean promised to do so. They set the meeting for today after school.

Doug turned into the driveway as Sean and Kevin approached the house. The youth sponsor, who operated a small quick-print shop in town with his wife, Jenny, had left work early to meet the boys. Once inside, Doug grabbed three Cokes out of the fridge. The three of them sat down to enjoy the drinks and talk.

In response to Doug's nonthreatening questions, Kevin talked about his parents' impending divorce, his loneliness, and his problems at school, mentioning that he had briefly entertained thoughts of ending his life. Sean was proud of his friend for being so transparent, even though he could see it was painful for Kevin to talk about the issues in his life.

"I would like to make a simple contract with you, Kevin," Doug said with an assuring smile. "You are very important to Sean and me and others in our youth group. I would like you to agree to call me immediately whenever the idea of suicide even crosses your mind. And I agree to respond to you immediately whenever you call and take time to talk with you. Will you make this contract with me?" Doug held out his hand for a handshake of agreement.

Sean glanced at Kevin, unsure how he would respond. Finally his friend said, "It means a lot that you would do that, Doug. I don't think I'll ever consider suicide again. But I promise to call you if I do. Thanks." Then he gripped Doug's hand and shook it. Doug promised to pray for him every day for the next few weeks.

Doug placed his Bible on the table. "I thought we could have a short Bible study on the topic of how God sees us. When we see ourselves as God sees us, we begin to realize how important we are to Him and others." Sean and Kev reached into their book bags and pulled out the small Bibles they carried to school.

"Turn to Jeremiah chapter thirty-one, verse three," Doug instructed. The boys flipped pages until they reached the passage. "Sean, why don't you read it aloud for us?"

Sean cleared his throat and read: "'The LORD appeared to us in the past, saying: "I have loved you with an everlasting love; I have drawn you with loving-kindness."'"

Doug asked, "According to this verse, how does God see us?"

Sean purposely held back to allow Kevin a chance to answer. "He loves us, so I guess He sees us as lovable."

"That's right, Kev," Doug said, smiling. "God sees you as lovable. He loves you with an everlasting love. He loves you no matter what you have done, no matter how miserable your life is, no matter how big your problems are, no matter how many mistakes you have made or sins you have committed. God never stops loving you . . . and He never will."

Doug referred to a few more verses that

emphasized God's abiding love. Kevin seemed most impressed by Isaiah 49:16: "I have engraved you on the palms of my hands."

He remarked, "Wow, God loves us so much that He has tattooed our names on His hands! I never realized God's love was that strong."

Sean and Doug smiled at Kevin's enthusiasm.

Next, Doug directed them to Genesis 1:27, Romans 8:3–5, 1 Peter 1:18–19, and Ephesians 2:10. Kev answered the question before Doug could ask it. "God must also see us as valuable. He created us in His image, just a little lower than the angels. He gave His own Son to die on the cross for our sins. He calls us His work of art, His masterpiece. And He has a plan to bless us and prosper us. That means we are very special to God."

The next set of verses focused on the Holy Spirit, concluding with Philippians 4:13, which Kev read aloud from his Bible: "'I can do every-thing through him who gives me strength.'"

Sean answered Doug's question this time. "These verses say that God sees us as useful to Him. He has given us gifts and abilities, He has sent His Holy Spirit to live in us, and He calls us to serve Him with the strength He provides."

Doug nodded enthusiastically. "We are not perfect, and sometimes we feel very incompetent. But God sees us as competent because His Holy Spirit lives in us. Second Corinthians five, verse nineteen, says that He has entrusted us with the ministry of evangelism. Isn't it amazing that God trusts imperfect people like us to bring others to Him!"

"I never thought about it that way," Kev put in, eyebrows arched in amazement.

Doug focused on Kev. "How does it make you feel, knowing that our perfect, all-powerful God sees you as lovable, valuable, and useful?"

Kevin considered the question for several seconds. Then he answered, "Part of me feels like God hasn't taken a very close look at me, because I don't see myself as lovable or valuable or useful to Him. But another part of me feels kind of honored that He sees me this way."

Sean posed the next question to Kev. "Who do you think sees you for who you really are: you or God?"

Kev thought about it, then he flashed an impish smile. "That's a trick question, Sean. Who would claim that they see things better than God does?"

Doug and Sean chuckled at his response. Then Doug said, "That's just my point, Kev. God doesn't make mistakes, and He doesn't have a vision problem. If He sees you as lovable, valuable, and useful—and the Bible says that He does—then that's what you are. Right?"

Kev smiled and shrugged. "Right."

Doug continued, talking to both boys, "I believe that God wants us to see ourselves as He sees us. That's how we gain the confidence to deal with the hard things in our lives. If we know that God loves us, values us, and desires to use us, we can get through anything."

Kev was suddenly sober. "Even the breakup of a family? Even the horrible death of a close friend?"

Doug reached out and touched his arm. "What do you think, Kev?" he responded, his face full of understanding.

Kev studied the kind faces of his friend and

his youth leader. "Yes," he said at last, "I think God can help me get through these things because I guess I am lovable, valuable, and useful to Him. I guess that running away from my problems is a bad idea if God thinks I'm okay."

"I think you're exactly right, Kev," Doug responded. "God thinks you're okay, and so do we."

Time Out to Consider

Kevin and other kids who entertain passing thoughts of suicide have two overarching needs. First, they need immediate, potentially life-saving intervention to neutralize their self-destructive thoughts and the circumstances that provoke them. Sean met this need by seeking Kevin out and providing comfort, support, and encouragement. If you suspect that a hurting friend is having suicidal thoughts, your first response is to meet his or her immediate needs for relationship, comfort, support, and encouragement. These elements should be supplied as soon as possible.

A second overarching need shared by Kevin

and others like him is for a new perspective of identity. People who consider suicide have a very low view of their value and worth. Kev considered himself a waste of space on the planet. No wonder he was tempted by suicidal thoughts. He did not consider his life worth salvaging. He lacked a sense of belonging, worthiness, and competence. This same distorted inner portrait is likely at the root of your friend's suicidal thinking.

Once you have begun to address your friend's primary need for relationship, comfort, support, and encouragement, make plans to deal with the second need. Help your friend to see himself or herself through God's eyes. You may want to do what Sean and Doug did: Take your friend through a Bible study that emphasizes that God sees us as lovable, valuable, and useful. Your friend must understand the biblical message of how God sees us so that he or she can begin to see himself or herself that way.

If you do not feel confident leading your friend in a Bible study, perhaps your youth leader or minister will help you, just as Doug Shaw helped Sean. The goal of the Bible study and ongoing input into your friend's life should be to emphasize these three biblical truths:

God sees us as lovable, giving us a sense of belonging. Just like everyone else, your friend needs to sense that he or she belongs to someone. We gain our ultimate sense of belonging when we understand that God loves us unconditionally, just as we are. John 1:12 declares that when we received Christ we became children of God. He accepted us as His sons and daughters and invites us to call Him "Abba, Father" (Rom. 8:15). The apostle John wrote, "This is love: not that we loved God, but that he loved us and sent his Son as an atoning sacrifice for our sins" (1 John 4:10).

God sees us as valuable, giving us a sense of worthiness. Our true worth is revealed in the fact that our loving God allowed Jesus Christ, His sinless Son, to die for our sins. The apostle Peter wrote, "For you know that it was not with perishable things such as silver and gold that you were redeemed . . . , but with the precious blood of Christ" (1 Pet. 1:18–19). Paul said, "God demonstrates his own love for us in this: While we were still sinners, Christ died for us" (Rom. 5:8). Impress upon your friend that if he or she were the only person on earth, God would have sent His Son to die for him or her. Your friend is worth the death of God's Son.

God sees us as useful, giving us a sense of competence. Paul was not boasting when he said, "I can do everything through him who gives me strength" (Phil. 4:13). He simply saw himself as God sees him: gifted and empowered by the Holy Spirit to serve God and others. God wants all believers to realize that He has given us certain physical, mental, and spiritual abilities and has equipped us to use those abilities successfully. God is so confident in our competence that He has called us to fulfill His Great Commission (see Matt. 28:18–20). Jesus said, "Apart from me you can do nothing" (John 15:5). But like Paul, empowered by the Holy Spirit we can do everything. What a sense of competence!

Do you see the importance of helping your friend see himself or herself through God's eyes? The scriptural understanding of our identity in

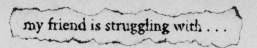

Christ may be a lifesaver. The more your friend realizes that he or she is lovable, valuable, and useful to God, the less likely he or she will be to consider suicide.

APPENDIX

Several times in this book I have mentioned the work of Dr. David Ferguson. David's ministry has had such a profound effect on me in the past several years that I want you to have every opportunity to be exposed to his work and ministry. David and his wife, Teresa, direct a ministry called Intimate Life Ministries.

WHO AND WHAT IS INTIMATE LIFE MINISTRIES?
Intimate Life Ministries (ILM) is a training and resource ministry whose purpose is to *assist in the development of Great Commandment ministries worldwide.* Great Commandment ministries—ministries that help us love God and our neighbors—are ongoing ministries that deepen

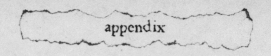

our intimacy with God and with others in marriage, family, and the church.

Intimate Life Ministries comprises:

- A network of **churches** seeking to fortify homes and communities with God's love;

- A network of **pastors and other ministry leaders** walking intimately with God and their families and seeking to live vulnerably before their people;

- A team of **accredited trainers** committed to helping churches establish ongoing Great Commandment ministries;

- A team of **professional associates** from ministry and other professional Christian backgrounds, assisting with research, training, and resource development;

- **Christian broadcasters, publishers, media, and other affiliates,** cooperating to see marriages and families reclaimed as divine relationships;

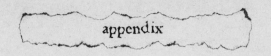

- **Headquarters staff** providing strategic planning, coordination, and support.

How Can Intimate Life Ministries Serve You?
ILM's Intimate Life Network of Churches is an effective, ongoing support and equipping relationship with churches and Christian leaders. There are at least four ways ILM can serve you:

1. *Ministering to Ministry Leaders*
ILM offers a unique two-day "Galatians 6:6" retreat to ministers and their spouses for personal renewal and for reestablishing and affirming ministry and family priorities. The conference accommodations and meals are provided as a gift to ministry leaders by cosponsoring partners. Thirty to forty such retreats are held throughout the U.S. and Europe each year.

2. *Partnering with Denominations and Other Ministries*
Numerous denominations and ministries have partnered with ILM by "commissioning" them to equip their ministry leaders through the Galatians

6:6 retreats along with strategic training and ongoing resources. This unique partnership enables a denomination to use the expertise of ILM trainers and resources to perpetuate a movement of Great Commandment ministry at the local level. ILM also provides a crisis-support setting to which denominations may send ministers, couples, or families who are struggling in their relationships.

3. *Identifying, Training, and Equipping Lay Leaders*

ILM is committed to helping the church equip its lay leaders through:

- *Sermon Series* on several Great Commandment topics to help pastors communicate a vision for Great Commandment health as well as identify and cultivate a core lay leadership group.

- *Community Training Classes* that provide weekly or weekend training to church staff and lay leaders. Classes are delivered by Intimate

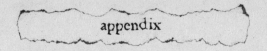

Life trainers along with ILM video-assisted training, workbooks, and study courses.

- *One-Day Training Conferences* on implementing Great Commandment ministry in the local church through marriage, parenting, or singles ministry. Conducted by Intimate Life trainers, these conferences are a great way to jump-start Great Commandment ministry in a local church.

4. *Providing Advanced Training and Crisis Support*

ILM conducts advanced training for both ministry staff and lay leaders through the Leadership Institute, focusing on relational ministry (marriage, parenting, families, singles, men, women, blended families, and counseling). The Enrichment Center provides support to relationships in crisis through Intensive Retreats for couples, families, and singles.

For more information on how you, your church, or your denomination can take advantage of the many services and resources, such as

the Great Commandment Ministry Training
Resource offered by Intimate Life Ministries,
write or call:

Intimate Life Ministries
P.O. Box 201808
Austin, TX 78720-1808
1-800-881-8008
www.ilmministries.com

Connecting Youth in Crisis

Obtain other vital topics from the PROJECT 911 Collection...

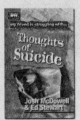

Experience the Connection

For Youth & Youth Groups

This eight-week youth group experience will teach your youth the true meaning of deepened friendships—being a 911 friend. Each lesson is built upon scriptural teachings that will both bond your group together and serve to draw others to Christ.

This optional video is an excellent supplement to your group's workbook experience.

As follow-up to your youth group experience, continue a young person's friendship journey by introducing them to a thirty-day topical devotional journal and a book on discovering God's will in their life.

Experience the Connection

For Adults & Groups

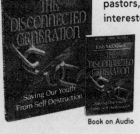

This watershed book is for parents, pastors, youth workers, or anyone interested in seeing youth not only survive but thrive in today's culture.

Book on Audio

This book, directed specifically to fathers, offers ten qualities to form deepened relationships between dads and their kids.

Begin your church-wide emphasis with an adult group experience using this five-part video series. Josh provides biblical insights for relationally connecting with your youth.

Experience the Connection

For Youth Workers

A one-on-one resource to help you provide a relational response and spiritual guidance to the 24 most troubling issues youth face today.

This handbook brings together over forty youth specialists to share their insights on what makes a successful youth ministry.

Contact your Christian supplier to obtain these PROJECT 911 resources and begin experiencing the connection God intended.

ABOUT THE AUTHORS

JOSH MCDOWELL, internationally known speaker, author, and traveling representative of Campus Crusade for Christ, International, has authored or coauthored more than fifty books, including *Right from Wrong* and *Josh McDowell's Handbook on Counseling Youth*. Josh and his wife, Dottie, have four children and live in Dallas, Texas.

ED STEWART is the author or coauthor of numerous Christian books. A veteran writer, Ed Stewart began writing fiction for youth as a coauthor with Josh McDowell. He has since authored four suspense novels for adults. Ed and his wife, Carol, live in Hillsboro, Oregon. They have two grown children and four grandchildren.